Real Estate Rock Star Foundations

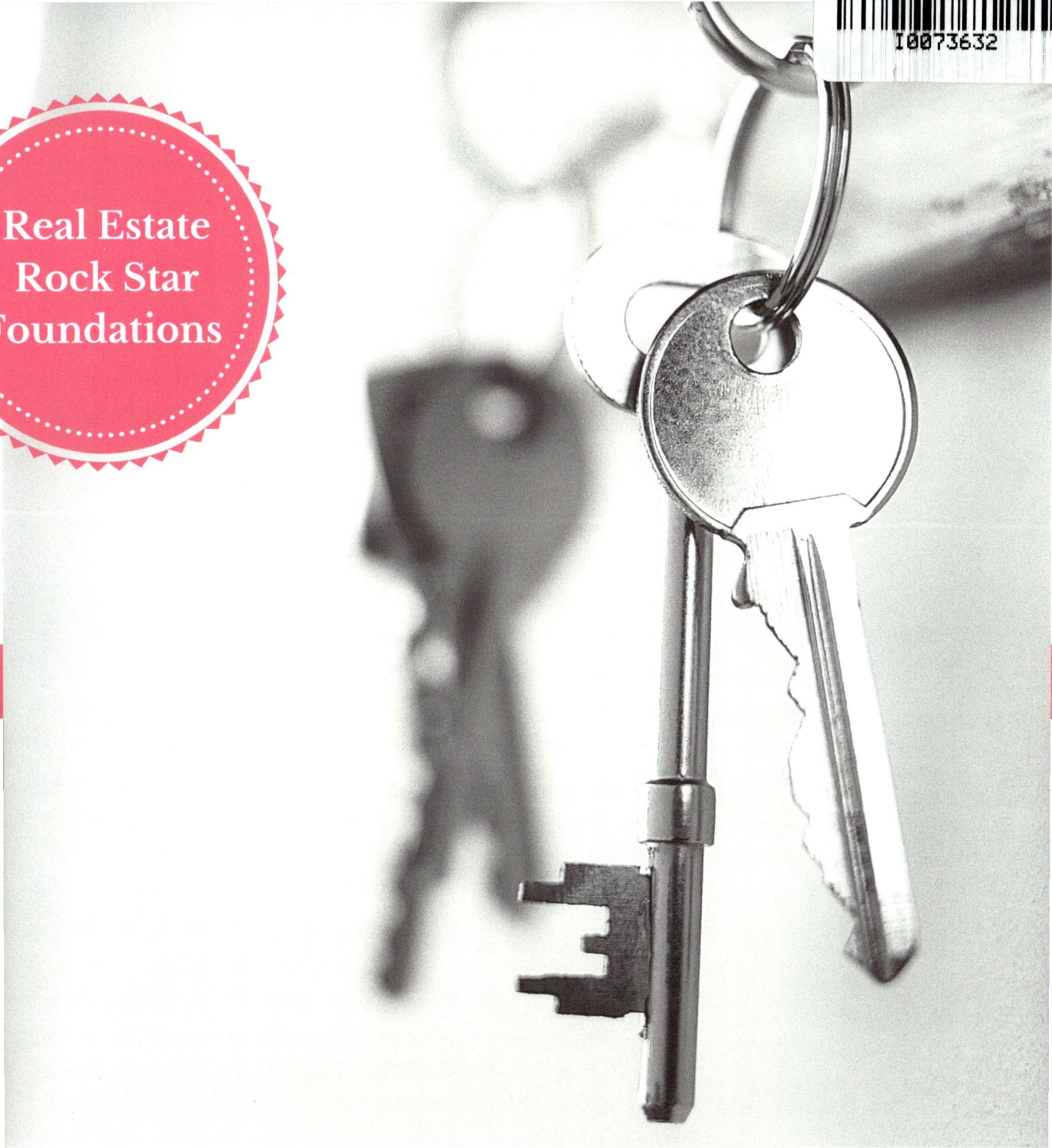

7 KEYS TO SUCCESS

HOW TO BECOME A REAL ESTATE SALES BADASS

Julie Fairhurst ~ RockstarStrategies.com

Rock Star Publishing
ISBN: 978-1-9995503-2-5

Workbook designed by Angelique Duffield
https://brightsparkwebsitedesign.com

BULK PURCHASES
For bulk purchases of this workbook,
please contact the author directly at:
julie@rockstarstrategies.com

7 KEYS TO SUCCESS

TABLE OF CONTENTS

INTRODUCTION

IS YOUR LACK OF SALES GIVING YOU SLEEPLESS NIGHTS?

I can totally relate! When I first started in sales I struggled daily and thought of quitting often. I wondered if I should get a "real job".

At the end of the day, I made the decision to stick with it...and I'm glad I did. My efforts paid off and with nearly 30 years as a full-time real estate agent, I'm grateful for the success I've had in my business, while working in a highly competitive industry. This career has allowed me to live a life that I thought was out of my reach.

Don't underestimate yourself! If I can do it, so can you. No matter what your past may be! I know, you've probably heard that before, but it's the truth!

LEARNING TO BECOME SUCCESSFUL IN SALES CAN TURN THINGS AROUND, AND I'M LIVING PROOF!

I went from standing in line at food banks and living off the government welfare system to becoming an award winning top sales professional.

With over $250 million in sales and working with over 2,000 clients, I was able to build the life that I dreamed of.

HOW WILL THIS GUIDE BENEFIT YOU?

By shifting your mindset, learning to "sell without selling", nurturing clients who say no, and discovering what taking action can do for you.

Most people are not just "born with it". You truly can learn these skills, and I'm sharing proven strategies that will help you build a thriving sales career so you can live your best life.

This is an opportunity to shift your success! I'm super excited for you to get started.

You can make notes in the spaces provide in this guide, and keep them handy to answer your discovery questions that you can look back on.

I wish for you all the success you desire!

Julie

1

CHANGING YOUR CORE BELIEFS & ADOPTING A SUCCESS MINDSET

CHANGING YOUR CORE BELIEFS AND ADOPTING A SUCCESS MINDSET

POVERTY OR PROSPERITY - WHAT MINDSET DO YOU HAVE?

Before I give you the strategies I've used for years to be successful in real estate sales, you will need to examine your mindset.

Your mindset, the one you have today, is doing one of two things for you:
1) It is serving you
2) It is hindering you

That's it, pretty simple. And I'm positive you know the answer to this, without having to give it much thought. You know you and you know your mindset. It can only be one of these two ways.

Depending on your family history, your past and the life you are leading now, you will know full well if your mindset serves or hinders you. Being honest with yourself is a key to your success.

WHERE DO YOUR BELIEFS COME FROM?

Have you ever given this some thought? Where did you get the beliefs that you have? Why do you believe what you believe?

What beliefs did your past generations pass along regarding money and success?

If you are like most of us, you just accepted the beliefs that were passed down by your previous generations. You adopted the ideas of your parents; your parents took the opinions of their parents and so on. Usually without ever questioning or realizing that they were doing it.

When I grew up, most of the time, well almost always, with our family surviving on the government welfare system, it was a negative environment. And with that negative environment came some strong shameful messages.

MESSAGES I HEARD WERE.....

Those damn rich people, they don't care about anyone but themselves. I'm not made of money. Money doesn't grow on trees. If it wasn't for you kids, I wouldn't always be so broke. We can't afford it. Who do you think you are? That's not us, our family doesn't live like that. People who have money are selfish. You can't trust people who have money, they will take advantage of you. Why work, the government just takes it. We never have enough. We have to cheat the system just to survive.

It was never the fault of anyone in my family for the way we lived. I never heard anyone say, "I had better go out there and get a job, so I can support my family." I grew up in a home of scarcity and lack. A home where no one ever took responsibility for anything and blaming others for our problems was the way to make them feel better.

Of course it was lies, lies told to cover up the shame and anger as well as passing the buck for responsibility. If you are not responsible, then you don't have to do anything to fix it.

When you live in that environment, year after year, you will naturally take on the beliefs of those who care for you. As a child there is no other choice but to accept what you are being told as true.

WHAT CAN NEGATIVE BELIEFS DO TO YOUR MINDSET?

- You feel ashamed
- You feel unworthy
- You think you don't deserve good things
- You think you can't achieve success
- You think you don't deserve money
- You are in a constant state of anxiety and depression
- You may wonder why bad things happen to you
- You may blame others for your situation
- You live in the past, unable to move forward
- You see yourself as a victim

These were some of the ways I was feeling and thinking while I was growing up. When I did try to do anything outside of my comfort zone, I felt like a fraud and was living in a state of anxiety that someone would be able to see the inside of me and call me out on being such a fraud.

DO YOU EVER FEEL LIKE A FRAUD?

If you do, then you understand how detrimental it is to your success in sales and in life. You don't have to continue to feel this way. Let's fix it!

DISCOVERY JOURNAL

What are some of the beliefs that have been handed down to you by your family? Write out as many as you can think of.

HOW DO YOU CHANGE YOUR CORE BELIEFS THAT ARE NOT SERVING YOU?

Your core beliefs are how you see you. How you judge you. How you see the world. If you are living your life with negative beliefs about yourself, money and success, your beliefs are most likely working against you.

BELIEFS ARE JUST THE THOUGHTS YOU THINK!

The good news is you can change your beliefs by being conscious of your thoughts. Pay attention during the day. How do you feel about yourself? How do you perceive successful people?

I'm sharing some past messages, I feel will work for you because they helped me develop a positive mindset. The good news is new thoughts create new beliefs.

- I am responsible for me
- I can do whatever I desire
- I see possibilities everywhere I go
- People are always ready to be helpful to me
- I am worthy and deserving
- People want to do business with me
- Money flows easily and freely to me
- I always have more than I need

CHANGING YOUR BELIEFS AND THOUGHTS IS IMPERATIVE FOR MOVING TOWARDS THE SUCCESS YOU DESIRE. HOWEVER, IT DOESN'T STOP THERE.

You can't just change your beliefs and then lay around the house watching TV all day long. Taking action is the next step in moving towards the life that you want.

I remember having a conversation with a girlfriend when she was complaining about not dating anyone for quite some time. She was not making any efforts putting herself out there to meet new people.

I told her, "you can't just sit there and wait for him to knock on your door. Get up and get out there."

It worked! She decided to take action and met her future husband at a local coffee shop.

DISCOVERY JOURNAL
Write out 10 positive messages for yourself, that will help you change your beliefs.

THE UNIVERSE HAS YOUR BACK, BUT IT CAN'T DO THE WORK FOR YOU. ONLY YOU CAN TAKE ACTION!

2

HOW TO "SELL WITHOUT SELLING"
BY SERVING YOUR CLIENTS' NEEDS

HOW TO "SELL WITHOUT SELLING" BY SERVING YOUR CLIENTS' NEEDS

HOW DOES HAVING TO SELL MAKE YOU FEEL?

For some of us, the thought having to sell something feels uncomfortable. You may hate the idea of selling or being thought of as a salesperson. No matter what you are selling (and real estate is no exception) if you fear sales, you are going to have a great deal of trouble being successful.

I was there! In the beginning of my sales career, I did everything I could to avoid the words "sales representative" or "sales person" on my business card. I was embarrassed to tell anyone I was in sales.

Selling for me was a tough job until I turned my mindset around.

If you are where I was right now, don't worry, we can fix that together so you can have a positive mindset around your sales career.

Most of us have had "bad" experiences with sales people. The sales people who come off arrogant and pushy, leaving you with a nasty dislike for people in the sales industry.

The good news is those sales people are a dying breed as the sales industry changes.

WHAT IS YOUR DEFINITION OF SALES?

Sales, I believe is the transfer of enthusiasm. If you're not enthusiastic for what you're selling, why would your buyer buy it? Your enthusiasm should be contagious!

When the buyer feels your enthusiasm, they will look at their potential new home differently. Instead of walking in with a mindset of "what's wrong ", their mindset will be "what's right".

Your task as the buyer's representative is to guide them so they can make the best decision for themselves and their family. Show your buyer that you are there to support them.

If there is a serious problem, point it out for them. However, if the carpets are green and not your taste, let the buyer decide, maybe green carpets work for them.

SELLING YOU IN YOUR MARKETING.

A soft approach to selling your services is through your marketing. When you are marketing a property, you are also marketing you. If you have crappy photos or bad sales copy, this is going to reflect on you. You are being advertised along with your properties!

Over the years, I have had homeowners contact me to sell their properties because they liked my advertising. Perception is everything when it comes to dealing with the public. Don't lose potential business because you allowed your marketing to look unprofessional.

WHAT ARE THEIR NEEDS?

Do you know what your potential buyers and sellers needs are? Not everyone requires the same marketing plan, or the same level of service.

It's important for success in your business that you understand what the needs and wants are in your area. What obstacles need to be overcome? What challenges are they facing?

No two clients are the same. Real estate is unique as everyone has different needs. Understanding the needs of buyers and sellers in your market, allows you to offer your services, tailor made specifically for them.

DISCOVERY JOURNAL
Make notes about what your prospective clients' needs are. Write as many as you can think of, it will help you when you develop your marketing plan.

SEE YOURSELF AS THEIR GUIDE.

Your prospective client will need you to guide them through the process of buying or selling real estate.

At times, we can forget how extremely overwhelming it can be when people are buying or selling real estate. You need to be their trusted advisor, someone they can lean on when the process becomes too much for them.

Have you ever been surprised by what you don't know? I'm amazed when I think of all the things I don't actually know anything about. Our world is changing rapidly, so how can anyone know everything that is happening at any given time?

Your prospective client is in the same situation as you, they don't know what they don't know.

This is why you're so valuable to them as their guide and advisor, you know what they want to know. This is your opportunity to guide them to an awakening of what they need and how you can help them. Help them solve the problem they may not even know they have.

MAKE IT ALL ABOUT THEM!

Have you ever had to sit through a conversation with a sales person who makes it all about themself? They go on and on about who they are and why they are so wonderful. You are their captive audience, thinking only about how you can escape. Don't do this to buyers and sellers!

- Be customer focused. Focus on them. Their needs and wants.
- Listening is important. Many people feel they are not heard. Be sure you hear your buyers and sellers. Let them know you are listening.
- Ask appropriate questions about what their needs are. When you ask questions, then give them an opportunity to answer, you prove that you care and are focused on their needs.
- Be honest. If you feel you are not a good fit for them, tell them. If you think they are making a mistake, tell them. The trust you build will go along way in your business relationship.
- Being honest and making it about them, will create a fan for life. This will give you an opportunity to ask for a referral, to pass your name along to someone they feel would be a good fit to work with you and who needs your services.
- Keep in contact with your new fan, if they are not ready to do business right away. When you feel the time is right to buy or sell real estate, you let them know. If you told them honestly that the time was not right before, and now it is, they will believe you and want to do business with you.
- Once you've mastered the art of making it about your prospective client, be sure to slide in about your services and how it can benefit them. They want to hear what you have to offer. Your services are the reason your meeting with them. Just be sure to remember the 80/20 rule.

LIVE BY THE 80 / 20 RULE: MAKE IT 80% ABOUT THEM AND ONLY 20% ABOUT YOU!

OFFER THEM SOLUTIONS OR OPTIONS

Have you realized what you have to offer is not going to work for the prospective client? Now is the time to be helpful. If you know someone who would work well with them, tell them and make the connection to the other agent.

Over the years, I've had other agents refer potential clients to me when, for whatever reason it was not working between them.

This can be a great opportunity to keep the clients happy and gain a referral. It should always be about the potential client and not about us.

Pass them along when appropriate to do so.

THIS IS YOUR OPPORTUNITY TO SHINE!

Network with others, be aware of what they have to offer and when you come across that potential client, if you think they would be a good fit, this is the time for a referral.

Work out a referral plan with others. Let's help one another along the way. There is nothing wrong with being paid a referral fee for referring business to others.

BUILD YOUR NETWORK.

Build a network of like minded people who offer various services and solutions. Discuss referral fees with them. What can you do to help each other?

Be sure to remember your rules for disclosing any referrals fees you do receive from referring business. Keep compliant and follow the rules.

Let's live in a mindset of prosperity rather than lack.

Think of others who would benefit with a referral for business. You would be doing a great service to your clients and others by having trusted business associates who you know will serve others as well as you do.

DISCOVERY JOURNAL

Write down who you could network with for referrals. Who would you trust even if you do not receive an incentive for your referral? Remember, what goes around comes around. Be an amazing resource for others.

3

ASKING FOR THE BUSINESS

ASKING FOR THE BUSINESS

WHAT YOU DON'T ASK FOR, YOU MAY NEVER GET!

Asking for the business can be uncomfortable for some real estate agents.

When you ask for the business, you may be pleasantly surprised at how many times you hear "YES". When you ask or don't ask, the universe will respond. Be sure you always ask.

"40% OF SALES PEOPLE SAY THAT ASKING FOR THE SALE IS THE MOST CHALLENGING PART OF THEIR BUSINESS!" ~ HUBSPOT.

LET'S LOOK AT WHY YOU DON'T ASK.

You've gone to so much energy, money and effort to get in front of your prospective client, why would you not ask? Here are a few reasons that may hold you back.

- **Fear of rejection.** This is huge, the fear of being told "no"? You'll have to wrap your head around this. Just because you hear "no", it doesn't mean they are rejecting you. No can mean a lot of things and in the end, it might not have anything to do with you.
- **Fear they will say "yes"!** If they say "yes", now what? Here you may have some fear around whether or not you can deliver on your promises?
- **You don't know how to ask.** Maybe you're asking the wrong questions? Not knowing how to ask can stop you from asking.
- **You are uncomfortable.** Possibly, you are unsure about sales? You may have be experiencing negative thoughts about sales and sales people. Maybe you had a bad experience with the sales process or a sales person in your own life?
- **Fear of putting someone on the spot or appearing pushy.** You may not want to put the other person on the spot by asking for the business.

YOUR PROSPECTIVE CLIENT WANTS YOU TO ASK... NO REALLY, THEY DO!

Would you be surprised to know that your prospective client wants you to ask them? Yes, they really do.

Why? Because they may be uncomfortable themselves, not sure how to move forward with your services or their purchase. They may be unsure of how to start the conversation with you.

So often we think it's about us. However, turn it around and make it about them. This will make it easier for you.

In real estate, it's all about your prospective client, always and never about you. You need to know when asking if they want to buy, proceed, continue or move forward, you are doing them a service and making it easier for them.

Sure, you will get some who will say, "no thank you". And when you do, that's okay because you gave them the opportunity and they were able to make their own intelligent decision as to what was right for then.

If you don't ask, you are not doing them or yourself any favours. Give your prospective clients an opportunity to ask questions, make up their own minds and give you their answer. This will only happen when you give them a chance by opening the dialogue with them.

REMEMBER... IF YOU DON'T ASK, THE ANSWER IS ALREADY NO!

HOW CAN YOU ASK FOR THE COMMITMENT?

Just ask. Simple isn't it? Just ask the question.

✔ **Be sure it is the right timing to be asking.** As you get comfortable asking you will be able to feel if it is the right time. Your intuition will kick in, be sure to listen to it.

✔ **Use a tactful, less daunting phrase.** I like to use, "Would you like to proceed with the paperwork"? When the conversation or presentation is over, it is an obvious question to ask.

✔ **Are you asking yes or no questions?** Don't ask questions that open more dialogue with the potential clients. At this stage, if they have all the information, you are looking for a one word answer, preferably a yes.

✔ **Be clear and direct as to what you are asking them.** Don't leave room for confusion. Remember you are looking for a one-word answer, so be sure to be clear.

✔ **Ask multiple times.** I have a program where I send out a letter to a prospect four times. Usually, I will hear from the prospect by the third letter. After the fourth time, if the prospect does not enter into business with me, I put them on my contact every six month list. 50% of my business has come from this strategy, it works, but you have to be consistent.

✔ **Practice makes perfect.** Practice asking. The more you practice, the easier it will be for you when the time comes. When you can ask with confidence in your voice, your prospect will take notice and more often than not, you will hear that yes.

HOW MANY TIMES DO I NEED TO ASK?

This will depend on who you are asking. You will feel and know if just one time is enough for this prospective client, or should you ask a further time.

There is a lot of information out there about how many times you need to ask. The most common advice would be 3 – 5 times before someone gives you a yes.

You may feel better knowing you're not the only one who has to ask multiple times for what you want

STAY IN INTEGRITY!

Never do anything out of character. This doesn't mean, I hate asking, so I will never ask. What it means is ask in your integrity and in alignment with your principles and values.

Legend says that Colonel Sanders from Kentucky Fried Chicken had to go through 1009 no's before he finally got a yes to his secret recipe.

Dr. Seuss's Mulberry Street was rejected by twenty-seven publishers before being accepted by Vanguard Press.

J.K. Rowling, it took two years to get the book, Harry Potter published. Twelve different publishers rejected the book before it ended up with Bloomsbury.

In the beginning of my sales career, I was told by my sales manager that I needed to be more aggressive when asking for business.

I thought, okay, I'll do what I'm told. Big mistake! I ticked off my prospective client because I was being pushy. I felt horrible as I was not working within my own integrity. Being pushing was not in my nature and I just made a mess of the situation.

Keep your ego and integrity in check when asking for the business. If it feels not right, then it's not right. Figure out what feels right for you.

WHAT DO YOU DO WHEN YOU GET THAT YES!

What you do next is get the signature, get the commitment in writing. Move forward with their yes to enter into the agreement with you.

Always use the word "agreement" rather than "contract". What is the difference? Nothing they are the same thing. The word agreement sounds softer.

DON'T EVER BURN A BRIDGE!

So you've asked, and it's 100% a no! They are not moving forward with you. Now what? Just leave it alone and respect their no and thank them for their time.

Don't take it personally. Even if they enter into business with someone else, they may come back to you at a later time, when they are ready or if they were not successful. I've had clients start out many times with others, only to be dissatisfied and come to me.

Always be kind and gentle with them, you never ever know.

DISCOVERY JOURNAL
Write down some thoughts you have of how you could ask for the business. In your way, within your comfort level and your integrity.

4

WHEN & WHY TO OFFER DISCOUNTS: IT'S YOUR BUSINESS DECISION

WHEN AND WHY TO OFFER DISCOUNTS

IS YOUR PROSPECTIVE CLIENT LOOKING FOR A DEAL?

Why would a potential client ask you for a discount?

✔ Don't believe in your value
✔ Needs extra money
✔ Does not understand your services
✔ Does not respect your time
✔ Likes to haggle
✔ Never pays full price
✔ Has succeeded getting lower price in the past

Discounting is a business decision that only you can make. If you are just starting out and you need to be able to say you have actually worked with others then you'll need to decide what you want to do. You are going to have to decide if you are going to give a discount to kick start your business.

If money is tight, you may want to give a discount to start bringing some business in and release some of the financial stress you may be carrying around. Giving a discount could go one of two ways. It could end up being a great business decision or a big mistake.

It's your business and it's your decision how to handle each and every aspect of your business, including selling your services.

Not everyone may be supportive. At times you may want to keep it to yourself, if you gave a discount rather than sharing it in a group or with others.

I gave a discount once to a seller. A friend from my office gave me a hard time about giving the discount. I felt stupid and not very good about myself at the time for giving it.

But hey! My office friend was doing just fine in her world and was not struggling. I on the other hand was a single mom with three young children to support. I needed the business.

Here I was, trying to make it in the sales world, where it can be super competitive where you are all alone. I was raising my three boys, with an empty bank account. I needed to survive and if that meant giving a discount to kick start my business, then that was what I was going to do.

After the negative reaction I received, if I gave a discount, I kept it to myself as much as I could.

HAVE THE CONVERSATION.

Be sure to have a long conversation with this potential client before you make your decision. The last thing you want is to discount your price and then have this client not respect you, your time, your money, your worth or your abilities.

However, you may feel after much consideration that you are willing to discount your price for this potential client, and it could be a good business decision.

THIS DISCOUNT WAS A GREAT BUSINESS DECISION!

Here is an actual situation where I made the decision, after careful consideration to give a discount.

A young couple, let's call them John and Susan, approached me and told me they liked who I was and how I did things.

However, they were very concerned about finances and moving to a new property. They told me they wanted to give me the opportunity first, but only if I would do it for the same prices as a discount agent they had spoken with. I had a look at what they were selling.

I liked them and decided I would give them the discount they asked for. And here's what happened...

1 I gave them the discount they asked for and sold their home without another agent. I received the entire fee for my services.

2 I sold them into a new home and received a fee for my services.

3 I sold their home, the one I sold them (gave another discount) and received a fee for my services.

4 I sold them into another new home and received a fee for my services.

5 They referred a relative to me. I sold the relative their very first home and received a fee for my services.

6 John and Susan sold their home to a relative of their neighbour. They called me to find them their new home and I received a fee for my service with a financial bonus from the listing agent

7 They referred me to their parents. I sold their home and received a fee for my services. I gave the parents a discount.

8 I sold John and Susan's home, the last one I had sold them into, gave them a discount and received a fee for my services.

9 I sold them into their forever home! Which was valued over $1 million dollars. I received a fee for my services.

I completed nine transactions with them. I had the privilege of working with an amazing couple over the years. I keep in contact and have watched their three children grow up.

All this because I gave them the discount they asked for. They referred me to their family and they continued to work with me because I did a great job for them.

You need to look at each situation individually and decide if you think a discount is going to work to your benefit or not.

WHAT IF YOU DON'T WANT TO GIVE A DISCOUNT?

If you have decided not to give a discount, here are a few strategies you can use to keep the potential buyers business.

- **Acknowledge the request.** Here is where you have the opportunity to sell yourself and your services.
- **Just say, no.** "No I'm sorry, I don't give discounts." But what can you do for them? This is where you may want to offer some sort of a win for the prospective client. You want them to feel valued by you.

- **Ask them "Why?"** You want to understand why they are asking for the discount. When you can understand their why, it may help you to discover what you can do to help them.
- **Compromise with the potential clients**. If you discount, what will that do for you and them?
- **You could ask, "What would need to happen to make my price worth what I quoted you?"** This will allow you to once again show your worth and give added value, if you choose.
- **You can respond with, "I hear you, the best services are often more expensive."** Here you are showing them, yes, it costs this much because my services are worth it.
- **Can you offer an added value?** What could you offer them to get them to say yes to working with you?
- **Is price really the only reason the prospective client is not moving forward?** Possibly the price issue is not the real or only issue.
- **Ask if they have ever used a service like you offer.** It could be that they are not fully aware of your offering. They may not have any idea of the cost or value?
- **Give examples of others who have used your services.** Demonstrate your value with happy, successful clients... whatever that may be for them.

DISCOVERY JOURNAL

Write down all the ways you would be able to handle a situation, when the client is looking for a deal.

5

SYSTEMS & FOLLOW UP:
EASY WAYS TO OUTPERFORM
YOUR COMPETITION

SYSTEMS AND FOLLOW UP: EASY WAYS TO OUTPERFORM YOUR COMPETITION

YOUR PROSPECTIVE CLIENT SAYS "NO", NOW WHAT?

What are you going to do with the prospect that is not ready to jump in with a heck "YES" and move forward? Are you going to be able to stay in contact with them?

Even if this prospect has entered into business with another real estate agent, you'll still want to stay in contact with them, when appropriate. The only time you do not stay in contact with a prospect is if they have specifically asked you not to.

So let's assume all is good and you're going to keep in contact with your prospect. Now what? How will you do it?

Here are a few ways you can nurture your relationship with your prospective clients. When they are ready to buy or sell real estate, you want them to think of you. Your name should be top of mind.

SYSTEMS ARE THE KEY!

You will need to develop a system that will work for your business, so you don't just let your leads float away.

DO YOU HAVE A CLIENT MANAGEMENT SYSTEM?

These systems are so important for your business. You may only have a few clients and think it is a waste of your time and resources to invest in one, but you'd be wrong.

You will have all the best intentions to follow up with your prospect, but then life happens! We will deal with what is right in front of us, now, today. The busier your get, when you finally come up for air, it could be days, weeks or even months since anyone has heard from you. Or worse, you have completely forgotten about that potential client and they, in turn, have forgotten about you.

You will need to find a system that works for you and your type of business. A system that will make your life easier and thus, keep your name at the top of your prospects mind.

I love the automation of client management systems in the sense of daily reminders for keeping in contact with my potential clients.

WHAT INFORMATION SHOULD YOU BE KEEPING?

Be sure your information collection does not appear to be an interrogation. Through your conversation, just make note of things that seem important.

Then one day, when they contact you, you can pull up their file in your system, prior to responding and it'll be like you are a long lost friend!

Your connection will be warm, not cold. And with a warm connection, you will be able to move quickly towards helping them with their needs.

MAKE NOTE OF ...

As much information as you can about your prospect! This will be helpful when you connect with them again.

- Their name
- Where they live
- Contact information
- Spouse's name
- Children's names
- Pet's name
- What they do
- Any hobbies
- Likes or dislikes
- Birthdates

Think of what you would say to a friend if you've not seen them in a long time. What would you know about them? What would you ask them?

There are lots of ways to keep in contact!

WHAT CAN YOU SEND THEM BY EMAIL?

First remember, depending on your area, be sure you know the rules with regards to contacting them. The last thing you want is a complaint to your Privacy Commissioner. Always be sure to ask them for permission to contact them prior
to sending out emails.

Once you have received their permission, then you can decide what type of information to use to keep them informed and your name in front of them.

You can use blogs, daily affirmations, positive quotes, newsletters or just general content. Be careful not be bombard them with too many emails, that will cause them to not read them and eventually unsubscribe you.

Whatever you send, make sure it's of value to that person. Always ask yourself, "will this bring value?" If no value, then don't send. Get creative and think outside the box.

WHAT CAN YOU SEND THEM VIA "SNAIL MAIL"?

Use your regular postal system. Now you may be thinking, well that's a lot of work. As well there will be a cost attached to mailing your prospect something to their address.

However, this is one of the most powerful ways to keep in contact. And guess what? No one else, or very few will do it. So that will set you apart from everyone else.

You want to be different from everyone else! Trust me, you send them something in the mail, to their home or place of business, they will remember you forever.

SEND THEM A CARD

Thank you cards...Thank you for meeting with me. Thank you for being so nice to me at that seminar. Whatever the situation was, a quick thank you note is personal and they will appreciate receiving it.

Don't we all like to be thanked and shown gratitude? Be sure to drop two business cards in with whatever you are sending. You want them to know who sent it and how to reach you. This is not the time to ask them directly for business. You are simply saying "thank you".

Sending two business cards is a very soft way of saying, "Oh, don't forget me and this is what I do". Also, they can keep one and give another to a friend.

You can also send them other cards. Birthday cards, anniversary cards, you get the idea.

And if you have collected and saved their information in your client management system, you can set up an auto-notification for a few weeks in advance. They will be so impressed and touched that you remembered them.

SUPER GREAT TIP! READY?
ALWAYS USE YOUR HANDWRITING, DO NOT TYPE OUT!

Thank you cards should always be handwritten.

This type of communication is meant to be personal and shows that you care enough by taking the time.

Handwrite the message in the card, the envelope address and even your return address. You may want to leave your business name "ABC Realty" off the return address, keep it as generic as possible. Nothing on it should be typed.

And lastly, a live stamp on it. Don't use bulk mail to send it, they will notice and this defeats the purpose.

SEND A SAMPLE OF YOUR BUSINESS.

You can send them offers in the mail or by email. It might be promotions you may have coming up, or a brochure for a property you are selling. Send them general market conditions for their area.

Yes it will cost something, so be careful to keep your costs in check. If it is small and cost effective, it can have a large impact.

HOW TO USE SOCIAL MEDIA

Join groups. Participate. Be seen, you need to be seen. Just joining is not enough, you need to engage in whatever is happening in the group.

Be real, if you like something, then like it. If you dislike something, be quiet, as quiet as a little mouse. Do not get caught up in anything that is going to cause you to look bad.

Even if you disagree and there is no problem disagreeing with someone or something. However, pick your battles wisely. I would strongly suggest that you stay out of the war and sit on the sidelines.

Protect your reputation. Don't allow tagging without your permission. Be careful what you allow to be posted. Keep things positive and avoid any controversy or controversial topics.

Social media can help make you or break you. You don't want to work so hard to build a following only to have it gone in a flash. Social media can be a very good friend or a nasty enemy.

It's not enough to just like things, give little comments as well. Remember to keep it short and positive. If you think that baby, doggies, kitties or whatever is cute, then say so. You want people to see your name and your comments. Be sure though to keep it positive.

Praise! Support! Thank! Give gratitude to people. Show them you care. Give your support as much as you can. Send them private messages if that is more appropriate. And be real.

People will remember you and appreciate your kindness. Be creative. Give value. Be helpful. Make it all about them. Show that you care.

People will remember how you make them feel. If you make them feel good, they will remember you with fondness.

DISCOVERY JOURNAL
Write down all the social media that you would like to join and come up with a plan to set up your profiles.

6

SETTING GOALS & BUILDING MOMENTUM

SETTING GOALS AND BUILDING MOMENTUM

WHAT DO YOU REALLY WANT?

Such an important question we should be asking ourselves on a regular basis. Where do I want to go? What do I really want?

I'm sure you've heard or have read about goal setting and how important it is for your future. You may have been told you should have 1-year goals, 5-year goals and even 10-year goals. I completely agree with that time frame for goals. It is super important to decide what you want in life and where you see yourself in the future. Most importantly, how you would like to see your life unfold.

I have set goals that were achievable as well as some that seemed more like a dream. I write my goals in my journal and reviewed them on a regular basis. It is amazing at how many of those goals and dreams I have already accomplished in my life.

Even goals that seemed unattainable, I thought I'd never have a chance of achieving, have come true for me.

I love this quote which resonates with me. It moved me to take positive steps forward.

"SETTING GOALS IS THE FIRST STEP IN TURNING THE INVISIBLE INTO THE VISIBLE." ~ TONY ROBBINS

I knew I needed to set goals for myself if I was going to be able to achieve the life I wanted to create. This was an important step that I knew was going to move me towards success.

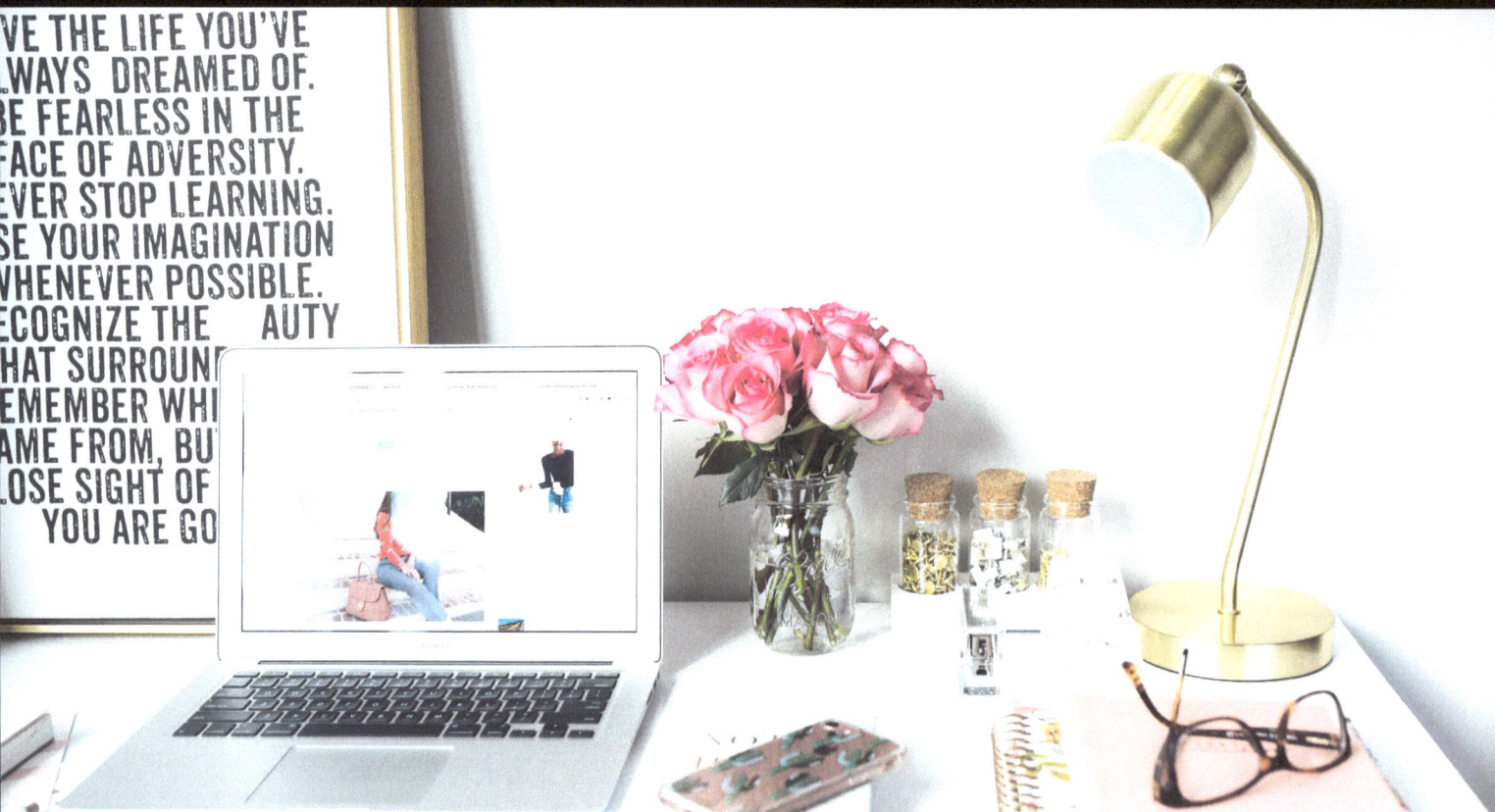

LET'S START WITH SHORT TERM GOALS.

What about today? It's fun to set those wild and crazy goals, to dream big. And, you should have those reach for the star goals, the ones that seem unattainable.

However, for now, let's focus on goals and dreams you want to achieve over a shorter period of time.

Here I want you to think on a smaller scale. Laser in on what you want to happen tomorrow, in 30 days from now, 60 days from now. Right up to 90 days from now.

Should you have those goals that you'll reach 10 and 20 years from now? For sure you should. Right now though, let's bite off a little bit at a time. If you are struggling to make sales, if your income is tight, if you're in a state of panic and frustration, then this is the time to get clear on your short-term goals and how you can achieve them.

I know your struggle, I was there! I remember being so broke, I couldn't even replace a headlight in my car, let alone put food on the table.

It can be hard to look at the big picture when you are living in fear of what is going to happen, not just in a year from now, but tomorrow!

WHAT CAN SHORT-TERM GOALS DO FOR YOU?

- Bring you immediate relief from your now situation
- Bring you motivation
- Help you organize your time
- Help to keep you on top of your resources
- Give you direction
- Gives you a sense of control
- Help you with clarity
- Build your confidence
- Bring you inspiration

WHAT DO YOU NEED TO HAPPEN SOONER RATHER THAN LATER?

This may not seem super sexy, but hey, this is where you are, so let's get some relief from your daily stress first before you start dreaming about that Mercedes Benz! Work in increments of 30 days to keep yourself on track and your goals attainable.

WHAT WILL YOU DO IN THE NEXT 30 DAYS?

- Write a business plan
- Have your branding completed
- Start a database
- Plan how much money will you earn from your business
- Hire a coach
- Attend a class / workshop / seminar
- Have professional photos taken

Be realistic when setting these short term goals, you don't want to set these goals so high that you can't reach them. You don't want it to seem like a struggle. Your short term goals should fuel your ambition. Get fired up and excited about the direction you are headed!

Short term goals are essential to get to those bigger goals. If you can obtain your smaller, shorter terms goals, that will set you up to obtain your massive more exciting goals.

The amazing value that your short term goals will bring you is keeping you on track to achieving the long term dreams for your life.

WHAT WILL YOU ACCOMPLISH IN THE NEXT 30 DAYS?

Will you....
- Have any clients or new clients
- Have your marketing pieces ready to go
- Have your sales copy written
- Have any sales in the work
- Have your presentation prepared
- Be making money

BUILDING MOMENTUM!

Nothing builds more momentum than seeing yourself achieving what you set your mind too. Even when they are small. A win is a win and you need those wins to keep your momentum and motivation flowing.

Once you've achieved one goal, then you achieve another goal and then another goal, you will feel unstoppable and your imagination will soar with new big and larger goals. You will believe that you can do it, you can achieve what you desire. And when you believe it, then you can do it.

Your goals will be bigger and bolder, because you will know that you really are worthy of all your hearts desires! You always knew it, maybe you just couldn't accept it for yourself? Accept that you can have it all!

WHAT WILL YOU DO IN THE NEXT 30, 60 AND 90 DAYS?

- Have your social media up
- Have your website up and running
- Taken a course that will help with your business
- Send information to your prospective clients
- Know how many clients are interested
- Have buyers and sellers working with you
- Be receiving income from all your efforts
- Bring on admin help

WHY IS IT IMPORTANT TO WRITE DOWN YOUR GOALS?

Forbes magazine quoted a Harvard MBA Program in which Harvard studied goal setting with their Harvard Graduate Students. This is what they found...

3% of the students had written goals
13% of the students had goals, but not written down, their goals were in their minds
84% of the students had no goals at all

10 years later, this is what the researchers found.

The 13% of students who had goals in their minds, but not written them down, earned twice the average amount of the 84% who had no goals.

The 3% who did have written goals, earned an average of ten times as much as the entire 97% combined.

The evidence is clear, if you write down your goals, you will have a greater chance to achieve them and ultimately be successful in all that you dream to do.

DISCOVERY JOURNAL

What are your dreams? Your dreams that you may be too afraid to share with anyone? Write the story of what your life will be like when you are living the life you dream.

7

TAKE ACTION!
START WITH LITTLE STEPS & BUILD YOUR SUCCESS ROUTINE

START WITH LITTLE STEPS AND BUILD YOUR SUCCESS ROUTINE

ARE YOU STUCK, FEELING OVERWHELMED AND NOT SURE HOW TO MOVE FORWARD?

When you're overwhelmed you may not be thinking clearly. Even the smallest of obstacles can look like mountains. You may feel like you are in a dark hole without a ladder to climb out.

I remember feeling that way myself, especially at the beginning of my sales career. Sitting at my desk, staring down at a pen and paper and feeling super overwhelmed and lost.

Oh sure, the manager gave me a bit of guidance and some tips on how to get out there and make a sale, but that was it. No hand holding or showing me the way. I was totally on my own. No one was leading the path. It was a scary time and I felt very much alone.

Have you ever experienced a time when you could feel that you were going it alone, it was up to you to figure it out?

ARE YOU FEELING STAGNANT?

Like water, you will become stagnant without movement. Taking action is your next step in moving towards the success and dreams you are longing for.

When you take action, you will find that doors will begin to open and opportunities will present themselves to you.

THE LAW OF ATTRACTION

Have you ever felt things just flowing in your life? A time when things just seemed to be working out for you?

That's when the law of attraction is working for you. You may think all you need to do is think positively and things will magically start to happen for you. Your mindset is certainly important, but it's only part of the process. One you have your mindset in check, then you need to start to take action.

I'm sure you have heard the phrase "**God helps those who help themselves.**" It's the same with the law of attraction and action.

When you start to take action, just doing something, anything you can do to move you towards what you want, the law of attraction recognizes your action and brings you things that will help you along your way.

WHAT WILL TAKING ACTION DO FOR YOU?

Taking action will move you towards your desires. Every action, even an action that you feel is not significant will start the energy to flow, no matter if it is a big or small action, it will move you towards your goal.

Jack Canfield, the author of Chicken Soup for the Soul says, "the universe rewards those who take action. When you take action, not only do additional resources come your way, but you also get feedback which helps you adjust your course and refine your approach.

Taking action is the one thing that separates successful people from everyday people in life."Creating successful habits begins with taking action. Success is a lifelong journey, and your new successful behavioural habits will be the tools that will keep you on the right track.

IS IT TIME FOR YOU TO GET INTO A SUCCESS ROUTINE?

Do you have a daily success routine? What does that routine look like? And if you don't have one, it's time to get on track with a success routine that works for you. However, for now, let's focus on goals and dreams you want to achieve over a shorter period of time.

Developing a success routine will get you closer to where you want to be faster then strong willpower, positive thinking or just trying to motivate yourself. Getting into a success routine and sticking to it will help you accomplish your goals and achieving your goals will give you the best motivation to keep going!

DISCOVERY JOURNAL
Now would be a good time to write out what motivates you to action. Write down the things you enjoy that you feel move you towards your success.

YOU ARE YOUR OWN BOSS!

As an entrepreneur, (and YES real estate agents are entrepreneurs) you don't have a boss standing over you with a big stick making you do certain things at a certain time. You are your boss. No one is watching to hold you accountable.

Many entrepreneurs work from home, as I do now. This means you are not in an environment that may inspire you or motivate you when you are feel down or overwhelmed. As an entrepreneur working from home, you may be spending a lot of time alone. It's important to find what motivates and moves you to take action and continue to take action.

START WITH THE LITTLE THINGS.

You are sitting at your desk, now what? What are the little things you can do to get your momentum started? What can you do to get started, that is easy and inexpensive?

If you are feeling overwhelmed and the cost of things are just too much, then do the little things. Anything you can think of. Action creates flow and energy, which develops into momentum.

- What is your why
- Why are you doing what you are doing
- What is the drive that got you here
- Who is your ideal client
- Will what you offer them
- What is your business story

- What do you have that connects with others
- How will you serve others
- What lights your soul up
- What can't you live without
- What are your unique gifts
- What causes you to not sleep

DISCOVERY JOURNAL
As you reflect on the questions above, make notes that you can refer back to which may give you some clarity.

TAKE ACTION WITH THE BASICS!

- Do you have business cards? if not get them designed and off for printing.
- Design your social media marketing and get started with promoting yourself and your service.
- What is happening with your website? Do you have one, if not get one on the go.
- Get your mailing list started. Who is going to be on the list? What will you send them?
- Research others who are successful at what you do? What can you learn from them?
- Are you ready to connect with your potential client? What will you say to them? What is the marketing material you will give to them?
- Do you have a filing system prepared to keep you organized?
- Do you have a database started to keep track of your clients or potential clients?
- Do you know your business inside and out? How can you transfer your enthusiasm to the potential client?

DISCOVERY JOURNAL
Write out ten action steps that can get you moving towards success today!

WHAT'S NEXT?

CONGRATULATIONS ON COMPLETING THE 7 KEYS TO YOUR SUCCESS!

You did it! Good for you! Now what?

Do you have the wisdom to ask for help? Maybe you don't need it, this was enough, you're on your way to the life you desire. I wish you all the success, love and happiness.

But if you want to skip the trial and error, follow a simple step by step process, and you're ready to dive deeper and learn strategies that can help you move more quickly towards building the lifestyle you want, I can help you along your path and show you that there is an easier way.

I'm the person that can get you there, because I was where you may be right now!

I invite you to share 30 minutes with me. Let's have a strategy session to discover your opportunity to shift your success.

If you'd like to speak with me you can schedule a time slot in my calendar on my website.

Book your strategy session today!

I believe a miracle resides in all of us and it happens at that moment when you decide to choose success over struggle!

Julie

CONTACT ME TODAY!